THE TALE OF PATRICK PEYTON

In collaboration with

Publisher	**REV. WILFRED RAYMOND, C.S.C.**
Writer	**PHILIP KOSLOSKI**
Pencils & Inks	**JIM FERN**
Colors & Letters	**MICHAEL LAVOY**
Flats	**ENID H. WILLIAM**
	MELVIN ROBLES
Cover Artwork	**JESSE HANSEN**
	MICHAEL LAVOY

www.FamilyRosary.org

JANUARY 9, 1909 - CARRACASTLE, IRELAND
WAAAAAA!!
PRAISE THE LORD!
IT'S A **BOY**!
WHAT WILL HIS **NAME** BE?
PATRICK WILL BE HIS NAME! AFTER THE GREAT **APOSTLE** OF IRELAND!

PA! SOMETHING'S WRONG WITH MA!!
BEATRICE, FETCH THE DOCTOR!
CHILDREN, LET US PRAY THE ROSARY AND ASK GOD FOR A CURE!
HAIL MARY FULL OF GRACE THE LORD IS WITH THEE, BLESSED ART THOU AMONG WOMEN AND BLESSED IS THE FRUIT OF THY WOMB, JESUS.
HOLY MARY, MOTHER OF GOD, PRAY FOR US SINNERS, NOW AND AT THE HOUR OF OUR DEATH, AMEN.
HAIL MARY, FULL OF GRACE...

WHAT IS IT, JOHN? HOW IS MARY?

THERE IS SOMETHING WRONG WITH MARY, SHE HASN'T RECOVERED FROM THE BIRTH.

I SEE SHE MAY HAVE CHILDBED FEVER, BUT SHE SEEMS TO BE ALREADY RECOVERING.
DID YOU DO ANYTHING TO HELP HER?

YES, YES WE DID. WE PRAYED!

NINE YEARS LATER...
CHILDREN! COME INSIDE NOW!

IT'S TIME FOR **DINNER**!

PATRICK, FATHER O'DONNELL NEEDS YOUR HELP AT **TWO** MASSES TOMORROW.

REALLY? I LOVE SERVING **MASS**! I CAN'T WAIT!

PATRICK, THANK YOU AGAIN FOR SERVING MASS. YOU REALLY ARE BLESSED WITH A DEEP FAITH AT SUCH A YOUNG AGE!

HAVE YOU EVER THOUGHT OF BECOMING A PRIEST?

YES, FATHER, I THINK ABOUT IT EVERY DAY!
I WISH SOMEDAY I COULD BECOME A PRIEST AND TRAVEL THE WORLD! I'M GOING TO BE A MISSIONARY!

YOU WILL MAKE A GREAT PRIEST SOMEDAY.

A FEW YEARS LATER...

I THINK WE SHOULD START WRITING **LETTERS** TO SEE IF THERE IS A **RELIGIOUS ORDER** THAT YOU CAN GO AND STUDY WITH

YOU ARE GETTING **OLDER** AND THEY CAN HELP YOU WITH MORE **SCHOOLING**.

YES! LET'S SEND A LETTER TO EVERY RELIGIOUS ORDER IN THE **WORLD**!

WEEKS LATER...

PATRICK! LOOK WHAT CAME IN THE MAIL TODAY!

WHAT DO THEY **SAY**? DID YOU GET **ACCEPTED**?

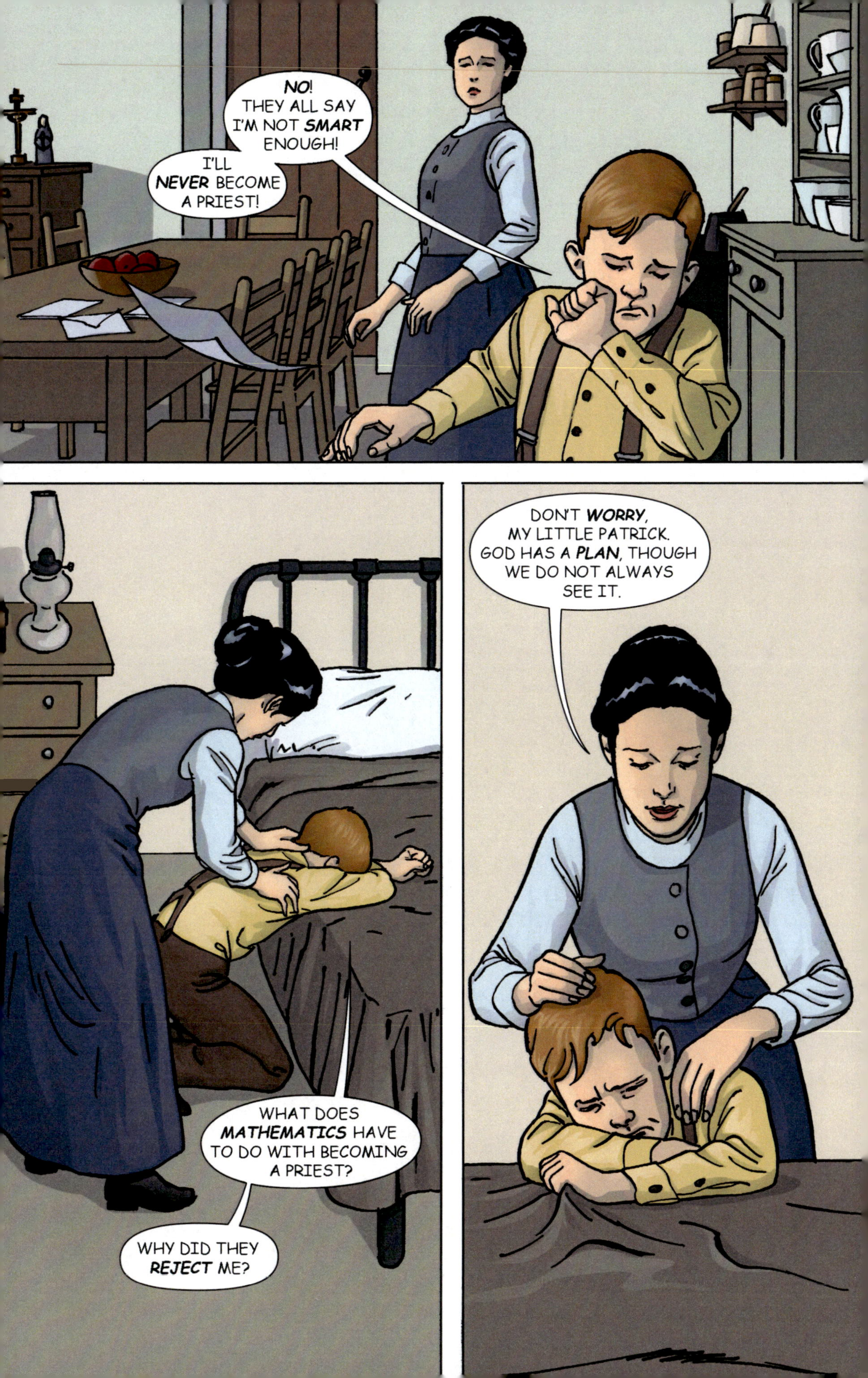

NO! THEY ALL SAY I'M NOT **SMART** ENOUGH!

I'LL **NEVER** BECOME A PRIEST!

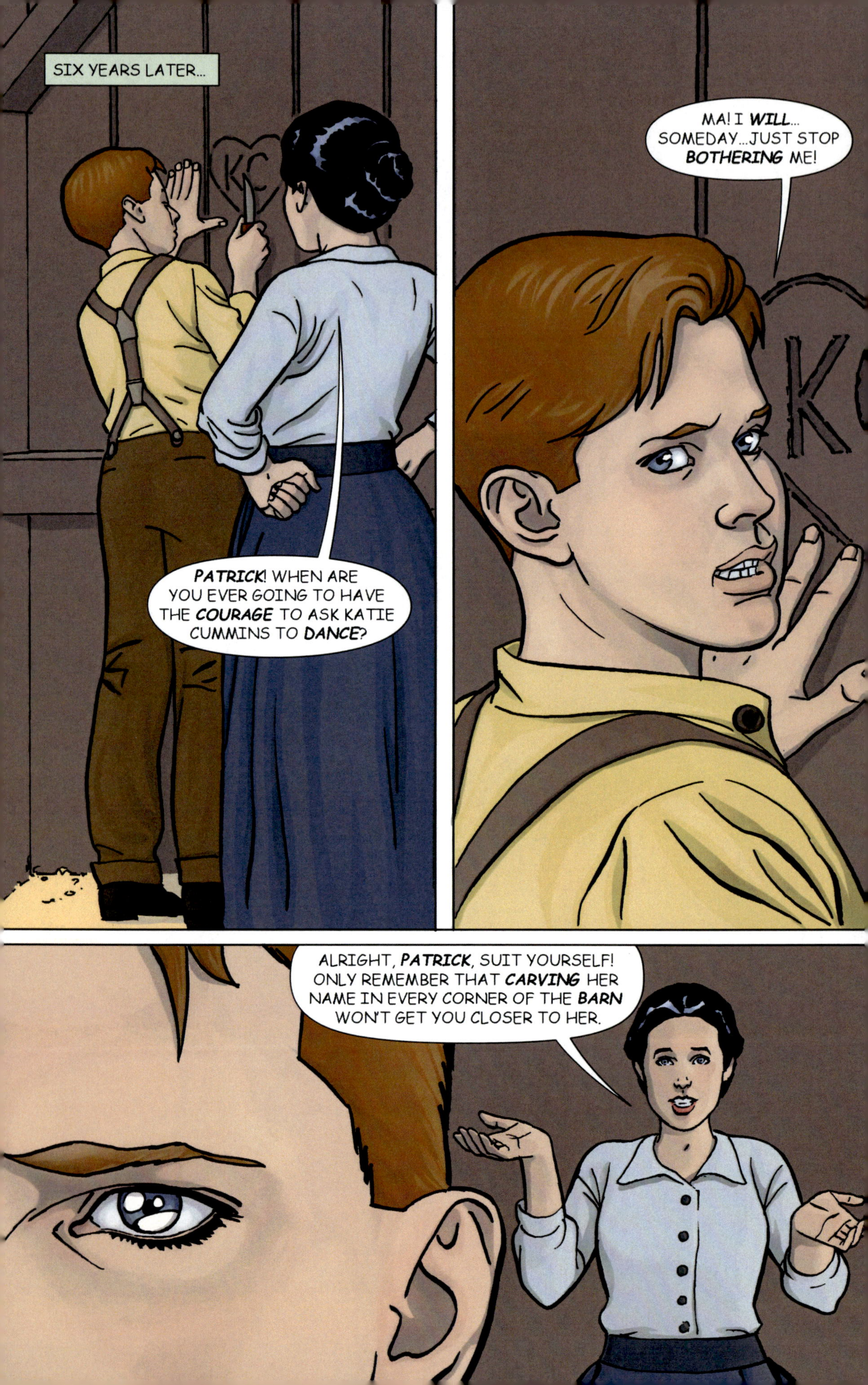

SIX YEARS LATER...

PATRICK! WHEN ARE YOU EVER GOING TO HAVE THE COURAGE TO ASK KATIE CUMMINS TO DANCE?

MA! I WILL... SOMEDAY...JUST STOP BOTHERING ME!

LATER THAT NIGHT...

I WANT TO **MARRY** HER...BUT I CAN'T EVEN **ASK** HER TO DANCE!

I HOPE SHE DOESN'T **LOOK** AT ME TONIGHT...I CAN'T **STAND** IT!

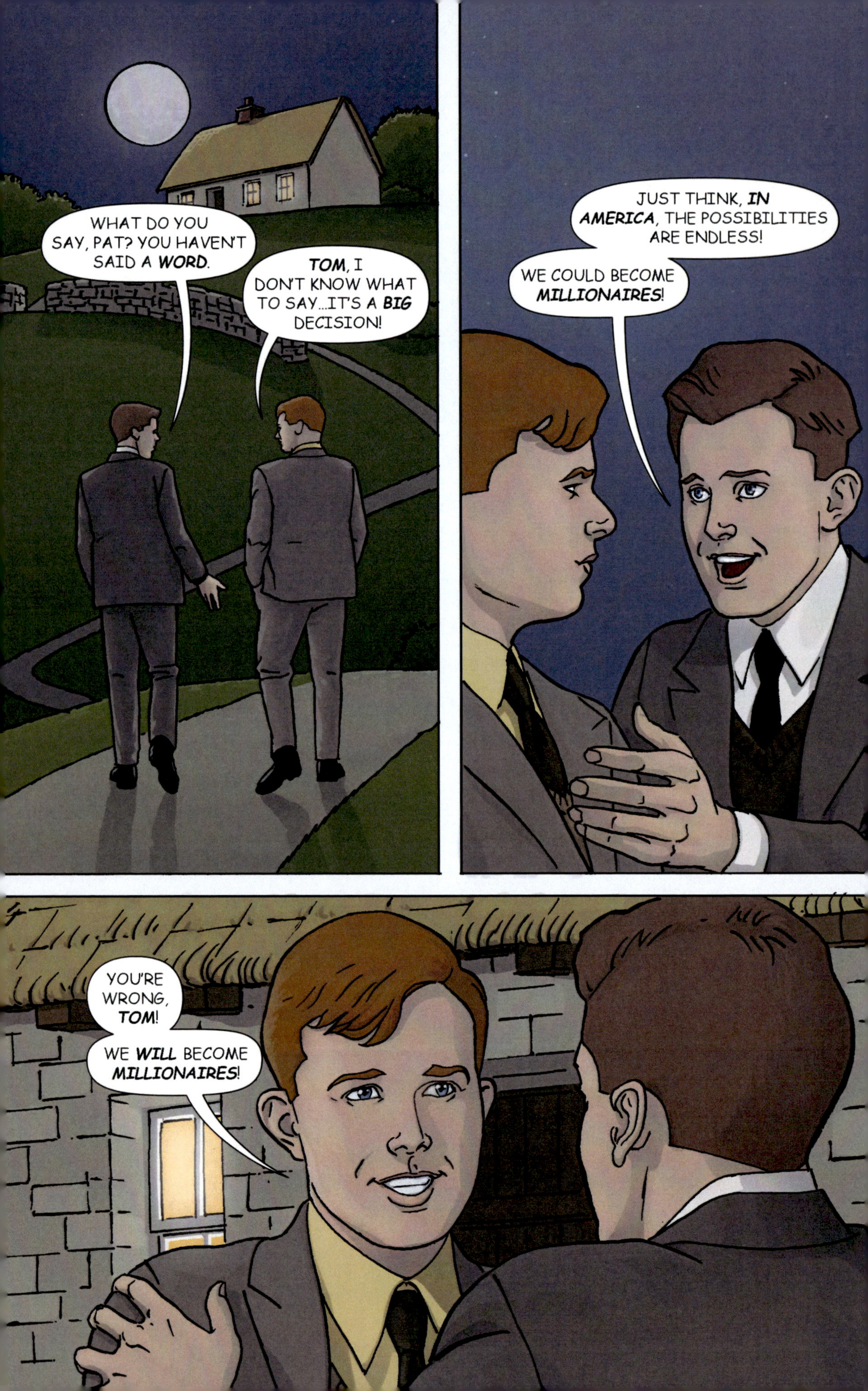

WHAT DO YOU SAY, PAT? YOU HAVEN'T SAID A **WORD**.

TOM, I DON'T KNOW WHAT TO SAY...IT'S A **BIG** DECISION!

YOU'RE WRONG, **TOM**!

WE ***WILL*** BECOME ***MILLIONAIRES***!

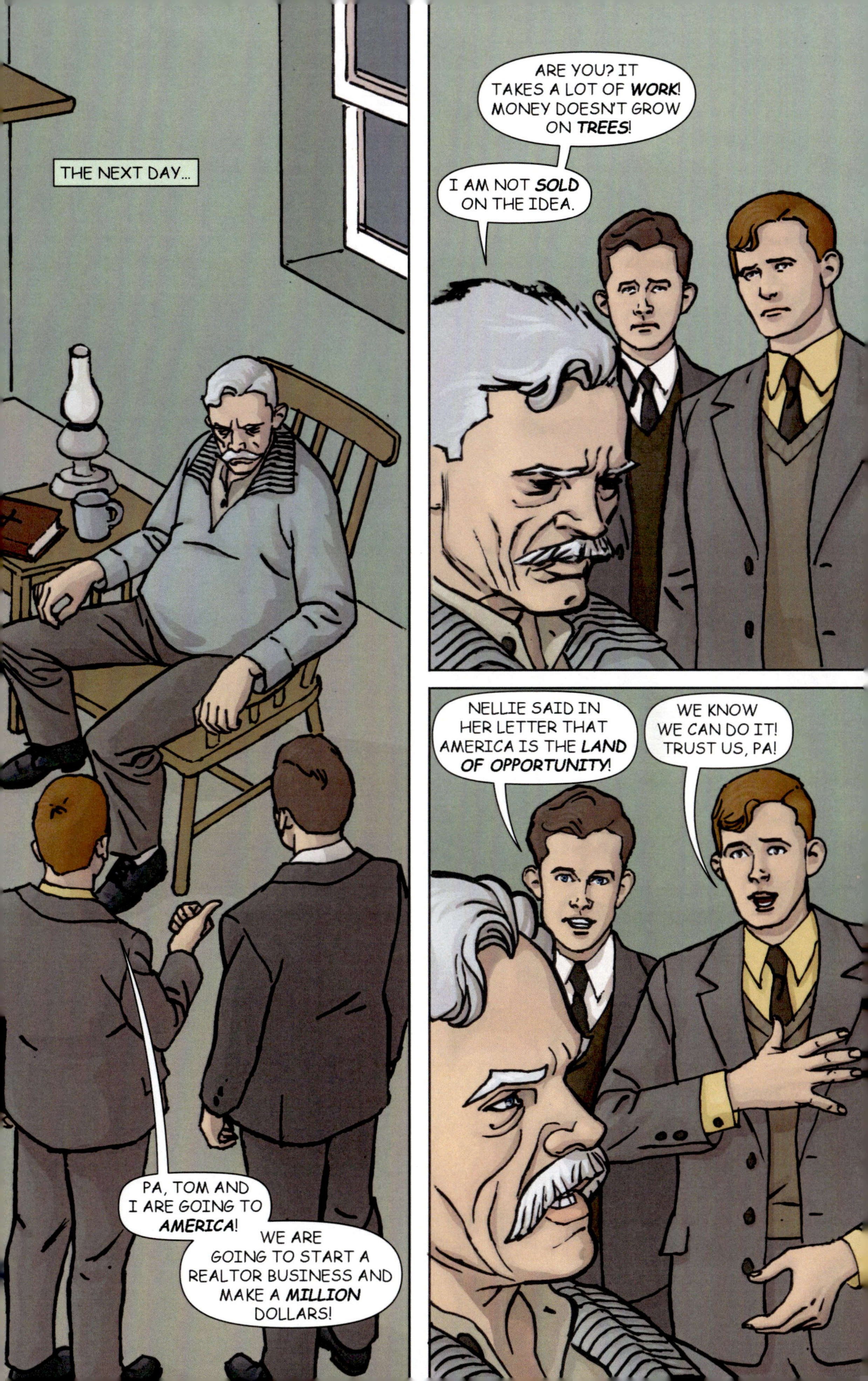

THE NEXT DAY...

PA, TOM AND I ARE GOING TO **AMERICA**!

WE ARE GOING TO START A REALTOR BUSINESS AND MAKE A **MILLION** DOLLARS!

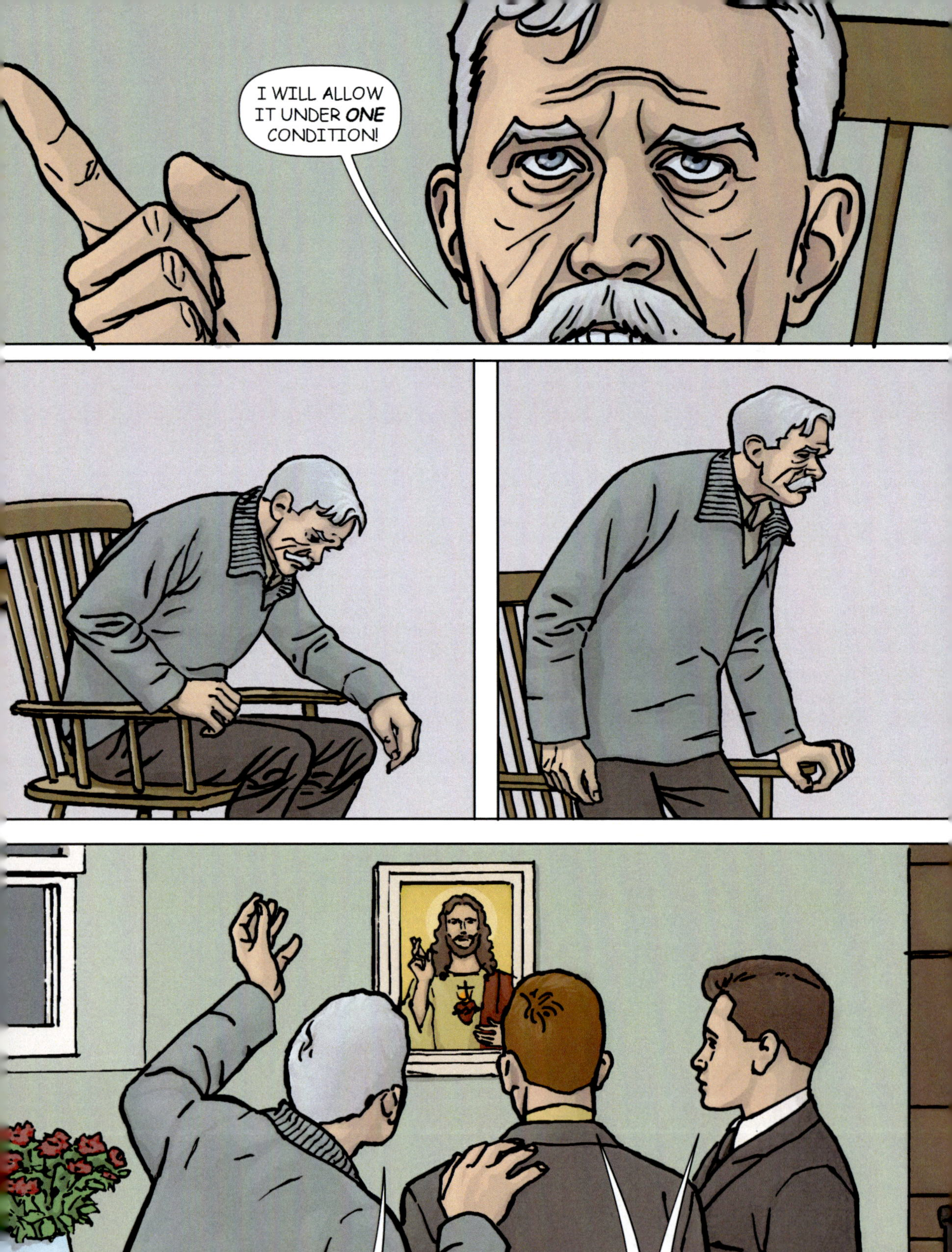
I WILL ALLOW IT UNDER ONE CONDITION!
MAKE ME A PROMISE HERE BEFORE THE SACRED HEART. YOUR FIRST RESPONSIBILITY WILL ALWAYS BE TO SAVE YOUR SOUL, AND SO I WANT YOU TO PROMISE TO BE FAITHFUL TO OUR LORD IN AMERICA.
YES, FATHER!

I AM GOING TO MISS YOU, MY **LITTLE PATRICK**!
DON'T WORRY, **MA**, WE'LL WRITE OFTEN.

AND SEND YOU **MONEY** ONCE WE MAKE IT BIG!

BYE **MA!**

WHOOOO WHOOOO
DID BEATRICE SAY SCRANTON WAS IN **TRANSYLVANIA**?
PENN-SYL-VANIA!!
WHAT!
PENN-SYL-VANIA!!
I SURE HOPE THERE AREN'T ANY **VAMPIRES** THERE!

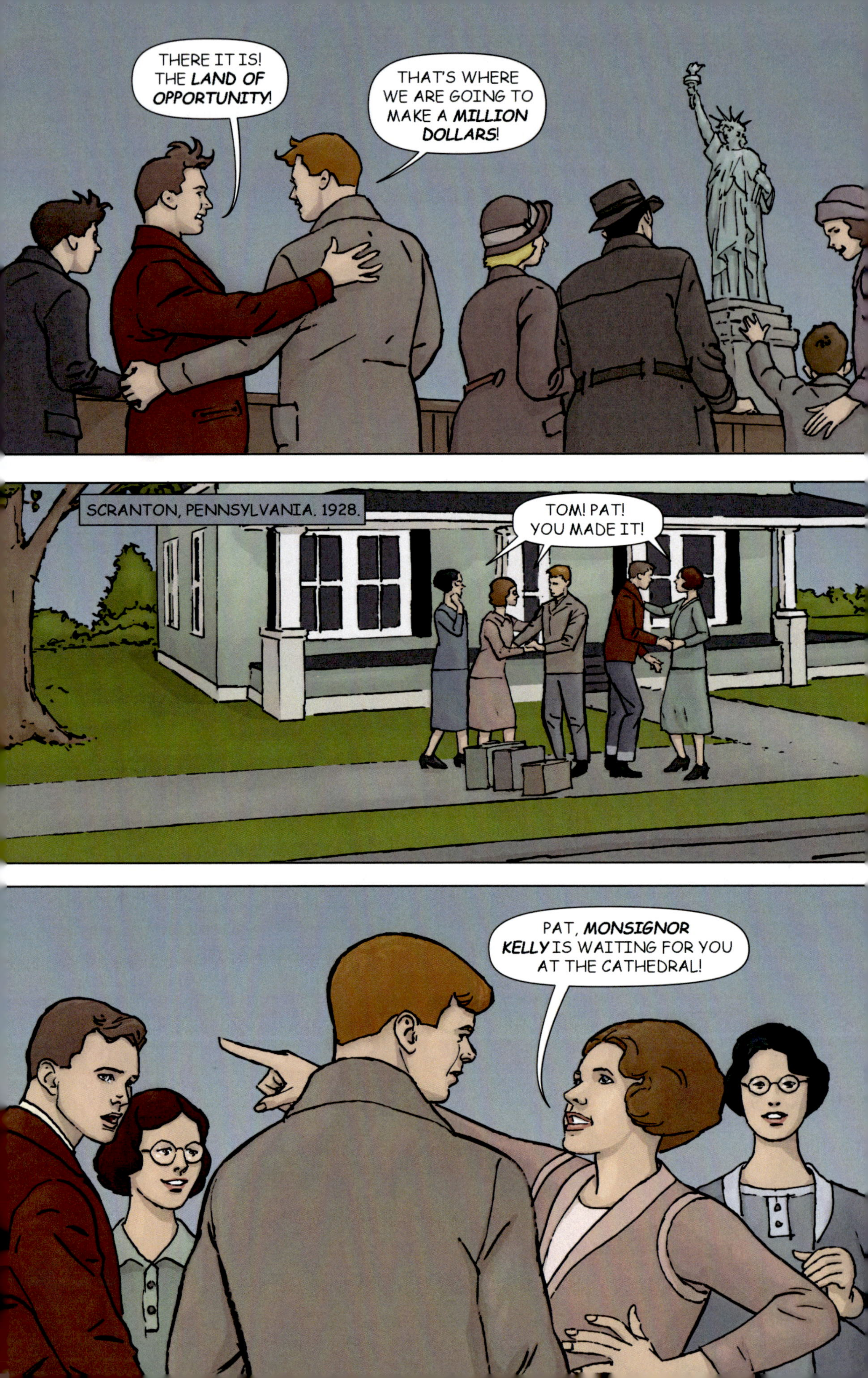

PAT, **MONSIGNOR KELLY** IS WAITING FOR YOU AT THE CATHEDRAL!

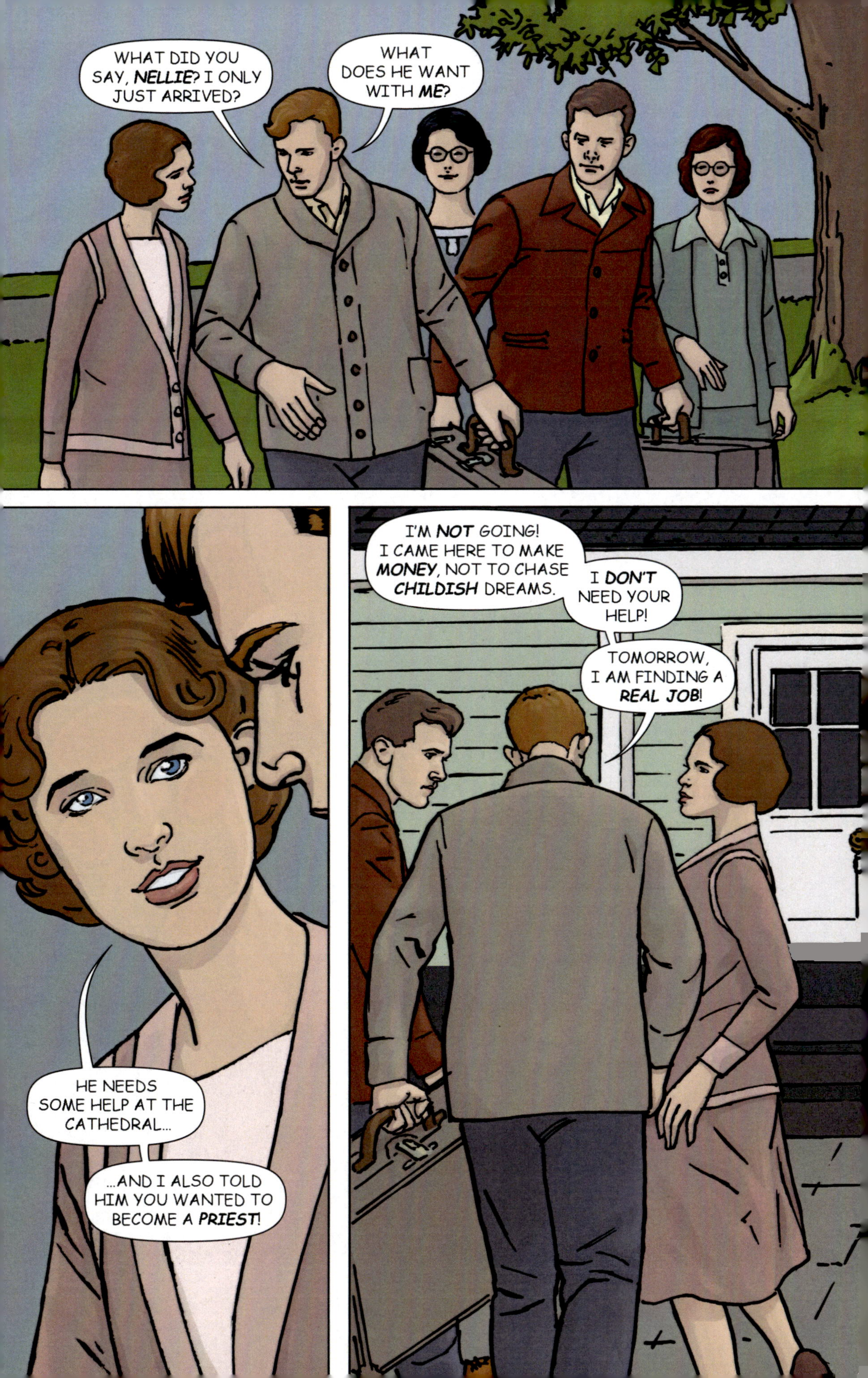

WHAT DID YOU SAY, **NELLIE**? I ONLY JUST ARRIVED?

WHAT DOES HE WANT WITH **ME**?

I'M **NOT** GOING! I CAME HERE TO MAKE **MONEY**, NOT TO CHASE **CHILDISH** DREAMS.

I **DON'T** NEED YOUR HELP!

TOMORROW, I AM FINDING A **REAL JOB**!

WAREHOUSE
WE'RE **NOT** HIRING!
TRY **DOWNTOWN**.
TODAY WILL BE THE BEGINNING OF SOMETHING **GREAT**!
SCRANTON THE ELECTRIC CITY
MANAGER OFFICE
SORRY **KID**, I JUST FILLED MY LAST OPENING.

NO OPENINGS!
TRY NEXT WEEK!
WE CAN'T HIRE ANOTHER PERSON!
I'LL LET YOU KNOW NEXT MONTH

I TRIED **EVERYWHERE**! EVEN THE NEW **PAPER COMPANY** IN SCRANTON DIDN'T HAVE ANY OPENINGS!
WHAT SHOULD I DO?
YOU **KNOW** WHERE TO GO!

AHH, YES, **PATRICK PEYTON**. WHAT CAN I DO FOR YOU TODAY?

MONSIGNOR KELLY, I NEED YOUR **HELP**.

I NEED A **JOB**.

LORD, WHAT AM I GOING TO DO WITH MY LIFE?
I THOUGHT AMERICA WAS SUPPOSED TO BE THE "LAND OF OPPORTUNITY"!
JUST ANOTHER DREAM WASHED AWAY—

WAIT! MAYBE I CAME HERE TO REALIZE A DIFFERENT DREAM!

MONSIGNOR KELLY, I KNOW WHAT I WANT TO DO WITH MY LIFE!

I'M GOING TO BECOME A PRIEST!

PATRICK SOON AFTER MET WITH HOLY CROSS PRIESTS AND WAS ADMITTED IN 1929, ALONG WITH HIS BROTHER THOMAS, TO THE HOLY CROSS SEMINARY AT THE UNIVERSITY OF NOTRE DAME IN INDIANA.
MARY, I GIVE YOU EVERYTHING, MY LIFE, MY FUTURE PRIESTHOOD.
HELP ME TO BECOME A SAINT.
COME ON, PAT, IT'S TIME FOR CLASS!
YOU CAN'T PRAY THERE ALL DAY!
I KNOW, TOM, BUT I NEED THE EXTRA HELP!
MARY'S GOING TO HELP ME WRITE THAT PHILOSOPHY PAPER!

PATRICK AND THOMAS GRADUATED FROM THE UNIVERSITY OF NOTRE DAME IN 1937 WITH HIGH HONORS AND THEN WERE SENT TO THE CATHOLIC UNIVERSITY OF AMERICA IN WASHINGTON D.C.
THANK YOU, **MARY**, FOR BRINGING ME HERE!
I AM SO CLOSE TO BECOMING A **PRIEST**!

COFF
COFF

NO, THIS CAN'T BE!

I CAN'T HAVE **TUBERCULOSIS**! I CAN'T **DIE**! NOT NOW!
I KNEW MY **DREAMS** WOULD **NEVER** COME TRUE!

AFTER CONSULTING WITH MY COLLEAGUES AND LOOKING AT YOUR **X-RAYS**...
...IT DOESN'T LOOK GOOD.
THE TUBERCULOSIS IS ADVANCED AND THERE IS **LITTLE HOPE** IT WILL TURN AROUND.

IS THERE **ANY CHANCE** I CAN GET BETTER?
YOU HAVE A **FEW MONTHS** LEFT ON THIS EARTH, MAKE GOOD USE OF THEM.
IT WOULD TAKE A **MIRACLE** FOR YOUR SITUATION TO IMPROVE.

I HEARD IT **DOESN'T** LOOK GOOD, PATRICK, AND WANT TO **ENCOURAGE** YOU.

FATHER HAGERTY, THERE IS **NOTHING** THEY CAN DO FOR ME!

THEY MAY NOT BE ABLE TO HELP YOU, BUT **OUR LADY** CAN!
GOD WILL **NEVER** SAY NO TO **HER**!

THIS IS MY CALVARY!

IT WON'T BE LONG UNTIL I COME HOME, TO BE WITH YOU, LORD.

UNLESS IT IS NOT YOUR WILL, LORD.
I WILL ENTRUST MY LIFE TO YOUR MOTHER AND ASK HER FOR A MIRACLE.

LORD, YOU CAN'T DENY ANYTHING THAT SHE ASKS OF YOU.
IF ITS YOUR WILL, I KNOW I WILL BE HEALED.

I KNEW IT! MARY ANSWERED MY PRAYER!
I AM HEALED!

THE DOCTORS COULDN'T EXPLAIN PATRICK'S MIRACULOUS RECOVERY. IT PAVED THE WAY FOR HIS ORDINATION ON JUNE 15, 1941, ALONG WITH HIS BROTHER THOMAS.
I **NEVER** THOUGHT THIS DAY WOULD COME!
ME NEITHER!
WHERE WILL YOU BE SENT?
I DON'T KNOW, BUT WHATEVER I DO AS A PRIEST, I WILL DO IT IN HONOR OF THE **BLESSED VIRGIN MARY**!
I **OWE** HER MY ENTIRE LIFE!

AFTER FATHER PATRICK'S ORDINATION, WORLD WAR II CONTINUED TO ESCALATE, AND FAMILIES ACROSS THE NATION STRUGGLED TO KEEP THEIR FAITH IN GOD.

MARY, THIS WAR **DIVIDES** FAMILIES.
HOW CAN I HELP THESE POOR FAMILIES STAY **UNITED** TO YOUR SON.

YES! THAT'S IT!
I WILL INSPIRE ALL **FAMILIES** TO PRAY THE **ROSARY** TOGETHER.
MARY WILL SAVE THE DAY!

THE INITIAL ROSARY CAMPAIGN WAS A SUCCESS! NOW FATHER PATRICK HAD BIGGER PLANS TO CONVINCE A RADIO STATION IN NEW YORK CITY TO BROADCAST A SPECIAL ROSARY PROGRAM.
BLESSED MOTHER, GUIDE ME!

ARE YOU COMING HERE FOR **FREE** TIME ON THE **RADIO**?
I AM... MY PLAN IS TO—
YOU ***CAN'T*** HAVE IT!
NOW ***SHUT*** THE DOOR WHEN YOU ***LEAVE***!

NOW ***WAIT*** A SECOND!
I CAME IN HERE NOT TO GLORIFY YOUR ***NETWORK***, BUT TO HAVE A HUSBAND AND WIFE ***PRAY*** ON THE RADIO AND ***INVITE*** OTHER FAMILIES TO PRAY.

DON'T YOU WANT TO SAVE ***FAMILIES*** OUT THERE AND BRING THEM ***TOGETHER***?!

WHEN YOU PUT IT LIKE THAT, I HAVE **NO CHOICE**!
I **WILL** AIR THE PROGRAM!

FATHER PATRICK SECURED THE SULLIVAN FAMILY TO HELP LEAD THE ROSARY, BUT HE STILL NEEDED A ***BIG MOVIE STAR*** TO CAPTIVATE A WIDE AUDIENCE.
HELLO?...CAN YOU TRANSFER ME TO MR. ***BING CROSBY***?

McCAREY
RIIIING!!!
RIIIING!!!

CUT!!!

MR. CROSBY! YOU HAVE A TELEPHONE CALL!

HELLO, THIS IS BING.

MR. CROSBY, I AM PUTTING TOGETHER A RADIO SHOW ABOUT THE FAMILY ROSARY...
...WOULD YOU JOIN US ON THE SHOW?

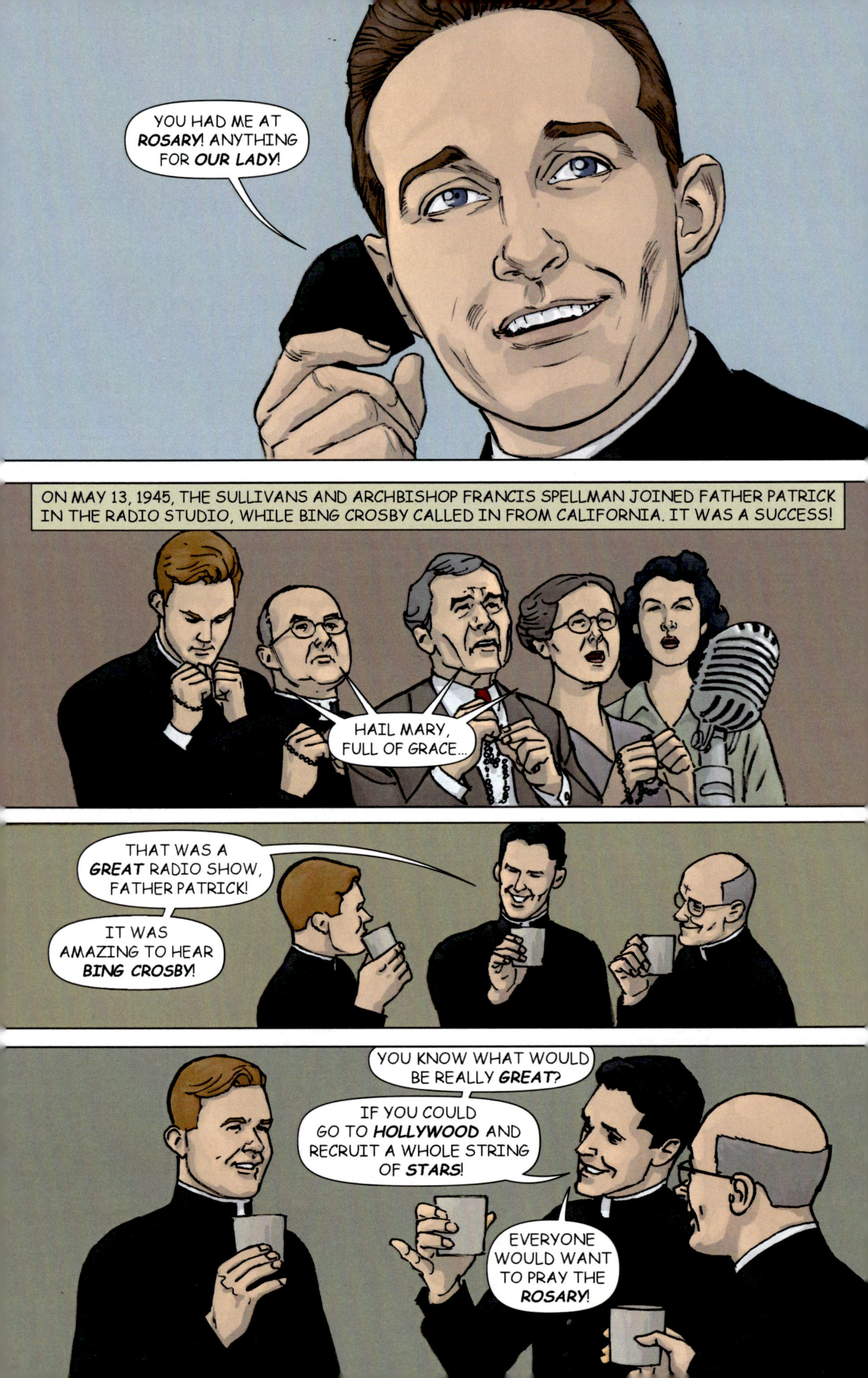

YOU HAD ME AT **ROSARY**! ANYTHING FOR **OUR LADY**!

ON MAY 13, 1945, THE SULLIVANS AND ARCHBISHOP FRANCIS SPELLMAN JOINED FATHER PATRICK IN THE RADIO STUDIO, WHILE BING CROSBY CALLED IN FROM CALIFORNIA. IT WAS A SUCCESS!

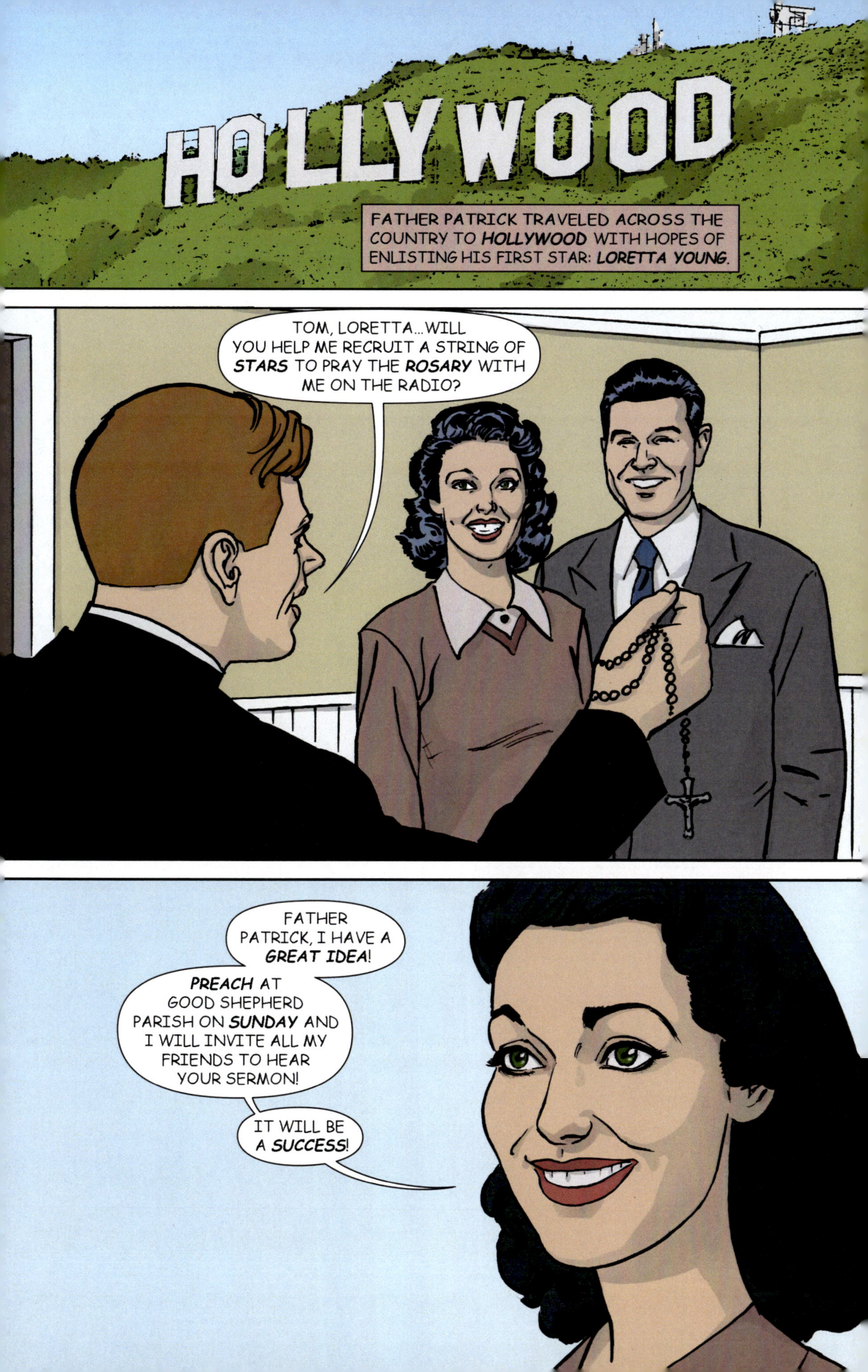

TOM, LORETTA...WILL YOU HELP ME RECRUIT A STRING OF ***STARS*** TO PRAY THE ***ROSARY*** WITH ME ON THE RADIO?

FATHER PATRICK, I HAVE A ***GREAT IDEA***!

PREACH AT GOOD SHEPHERD PARISH ON ***SUNDAY*** AND I WILL INVITE ALL MY FRIENDS TO HEAR YOUR SERMON!

IT WILL BE A ***SUCCESS***!

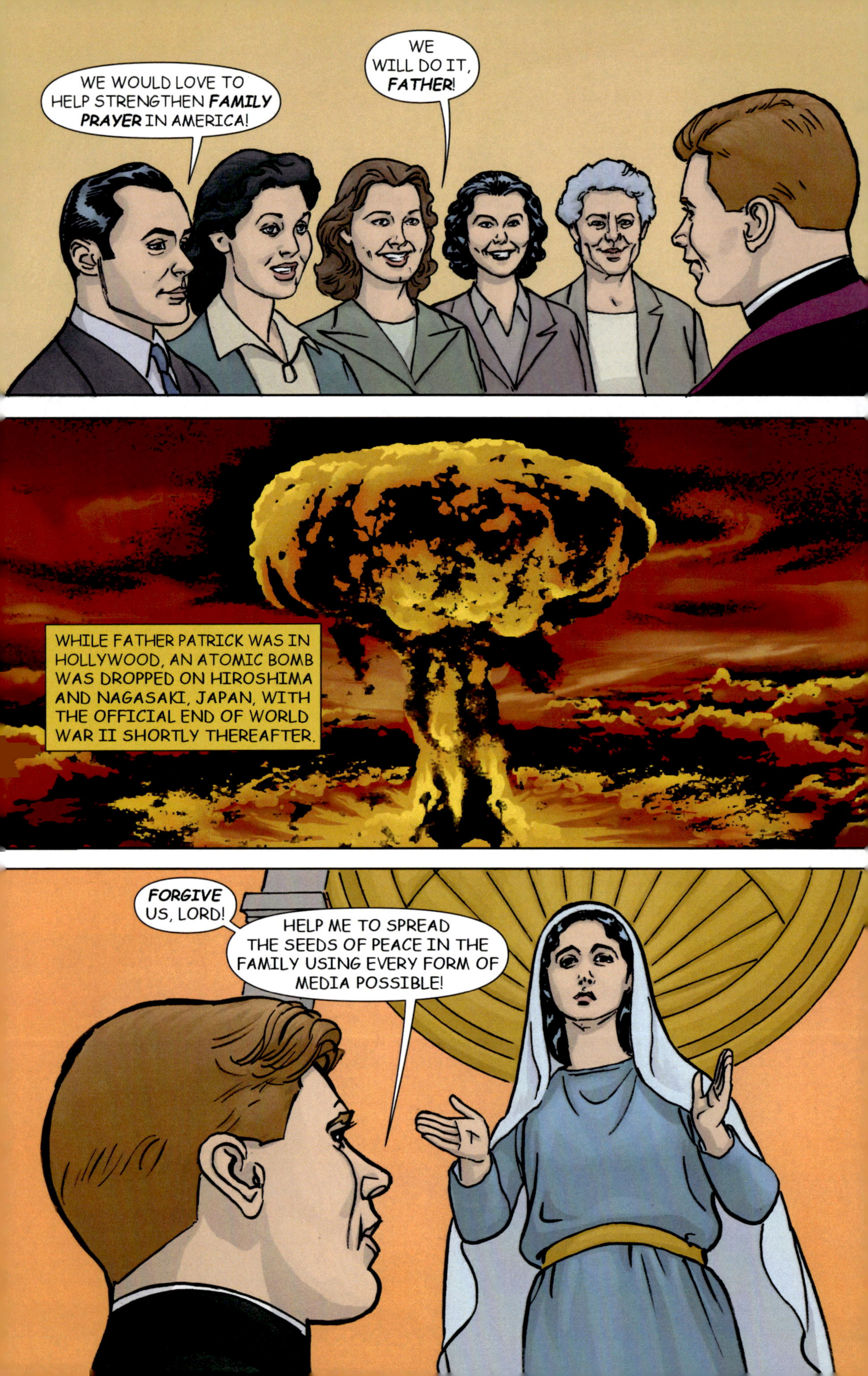

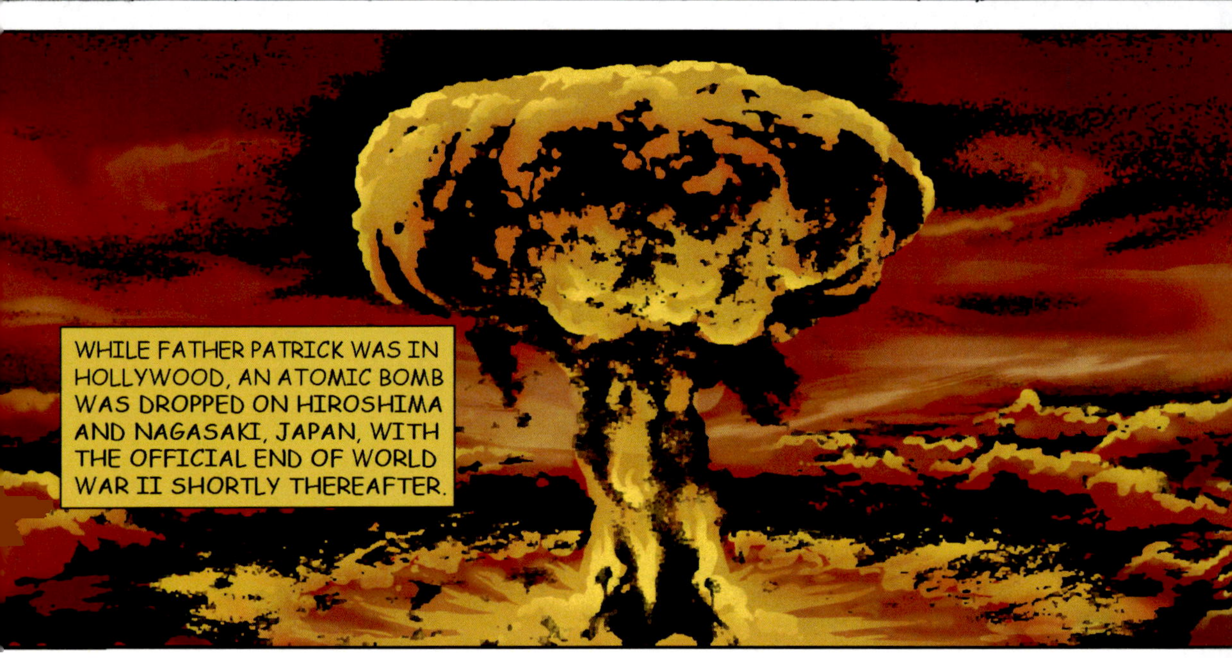

FORGIVE US, LORD!

HELP ME TO SPREAD THE SEEDS OF PEACE IN THE FAMILY USING EVERY FORM OF MEDIA POSSIBLE!

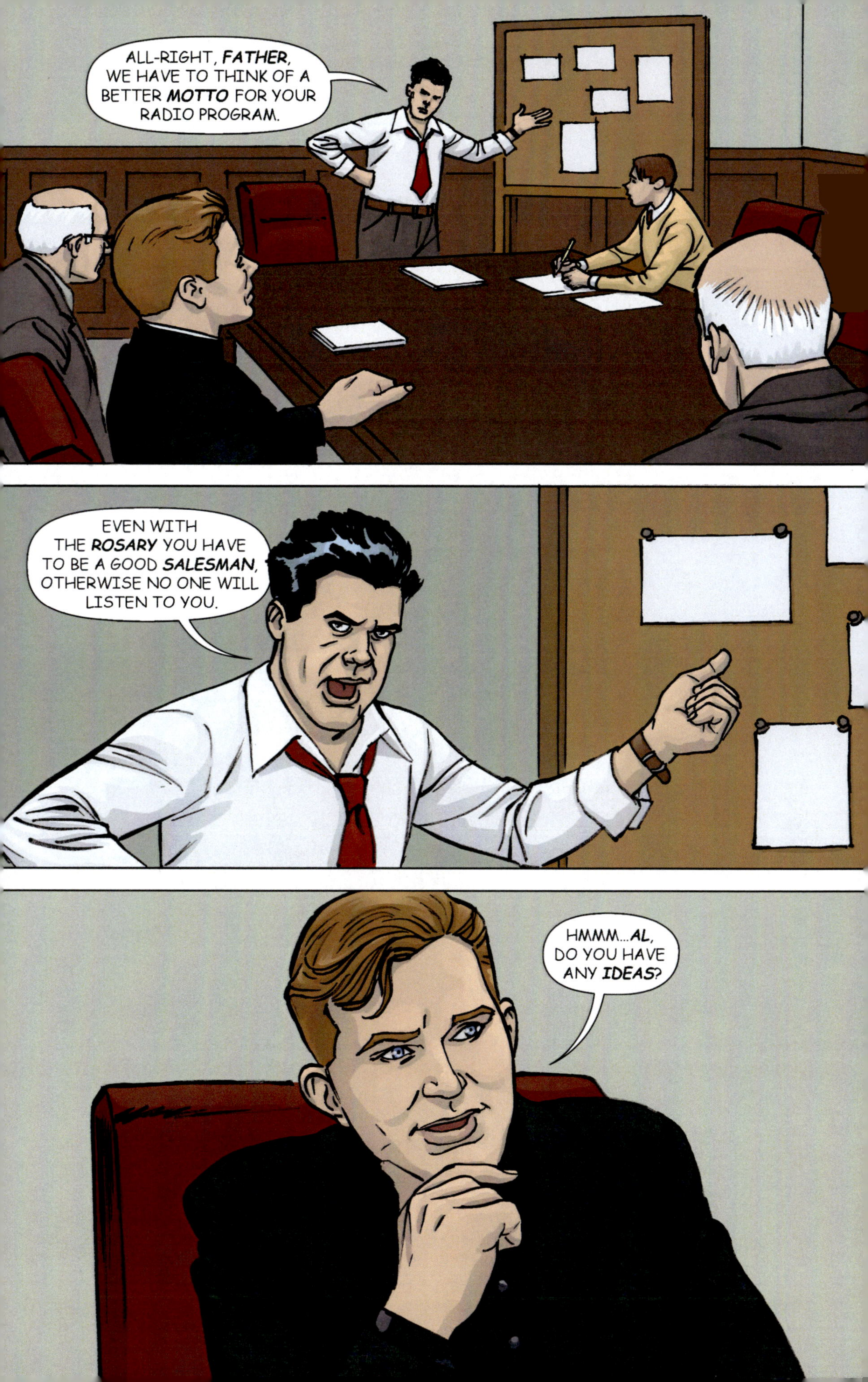

ALL-RIGHT, **FATHER**, WE HAVE TO THINK OF A BETTER **MOTTO** FOR YOUR RADIO PROGRAM.

HMMM...**AL**, DO YOU HAVE ANY **IDEAS**?

HEY **JIMMY**, WHAT DID WE COME-UP WITH THE OTHER DAY.

THE FAMILY THAT **PRAYS** TOGETHER, **STAYS** TOGETHER...

...A WORLD AT **PRAYER** IS A WORLD AT **PEACE**.

MR. SCALPONE, THOSE ARE **PERFECT**! PROFOUND AND EASY TO REMEMBER!

OUR LADY WILL BE HAPPY WITH THESE MOTTOS!

BEGINNING IN 1949, FATHER PATRICK EXPANDED HIS ROSARY MINISTRY TO INCLUDE SHORT FILMS ON THE MYSTERIES OF THE ROSARY, WHICH LATER EXPANDED TO FILMS ON OTHER RELIGIOUS TOPICS.
ACTION!
ROLLING!
FATHER PATRICK'S FILMS ALSO GAVE SEVERAL FAMOUS ***ACTORS*** AND ***DIRECTORS*** THEIR FIRST MOVIE CREDITS.

THE SHORT FILM **HILL NUMBER ONE** PRODUCED IN 1951 WAS ONE OF FATHER PATRICK'S MOST SUCCESSFUL PRODUCTIONS, FEATURING JAMES DEAN AS JOHN THE APOSTLE.
PETER!
WHAT IS IT **MARY**? WHAT HAS **FRIGHTENED** YOU?

PETER! THE TOMB IS **EMPTY**!

HE HAS RISEN, JOHN! I DO NOT UNDERSTAND!
HE WILL ENLIGHTEN US, PETER.
COME, WE WILL **SPREAD** THESE GOOD TIDINGS, **QUICKLY**!

SCENE Empty Tomb
TAKE 2
SOUND John
PROD. Hill Number One
DIRECTOR Arthur Pierson
CAMERA Camera One
DATE 1951
EXT.
INT.

CUT! THAT'S A WRAP!

YOU DID A GREAT JOB, ***JAMES!*** YOUR PORTRAYAL OF JOHN THE APOSTLE WAS ***EXCELLENT!***

YOU ARE GOING TO GO ***FAR*** IN THE ***MOVIE*** BUSINESS!

THANKS ***FATHER!*** I WILL ALWAYS REMEMBER THIS AS MY ***FIRST ROLE!***

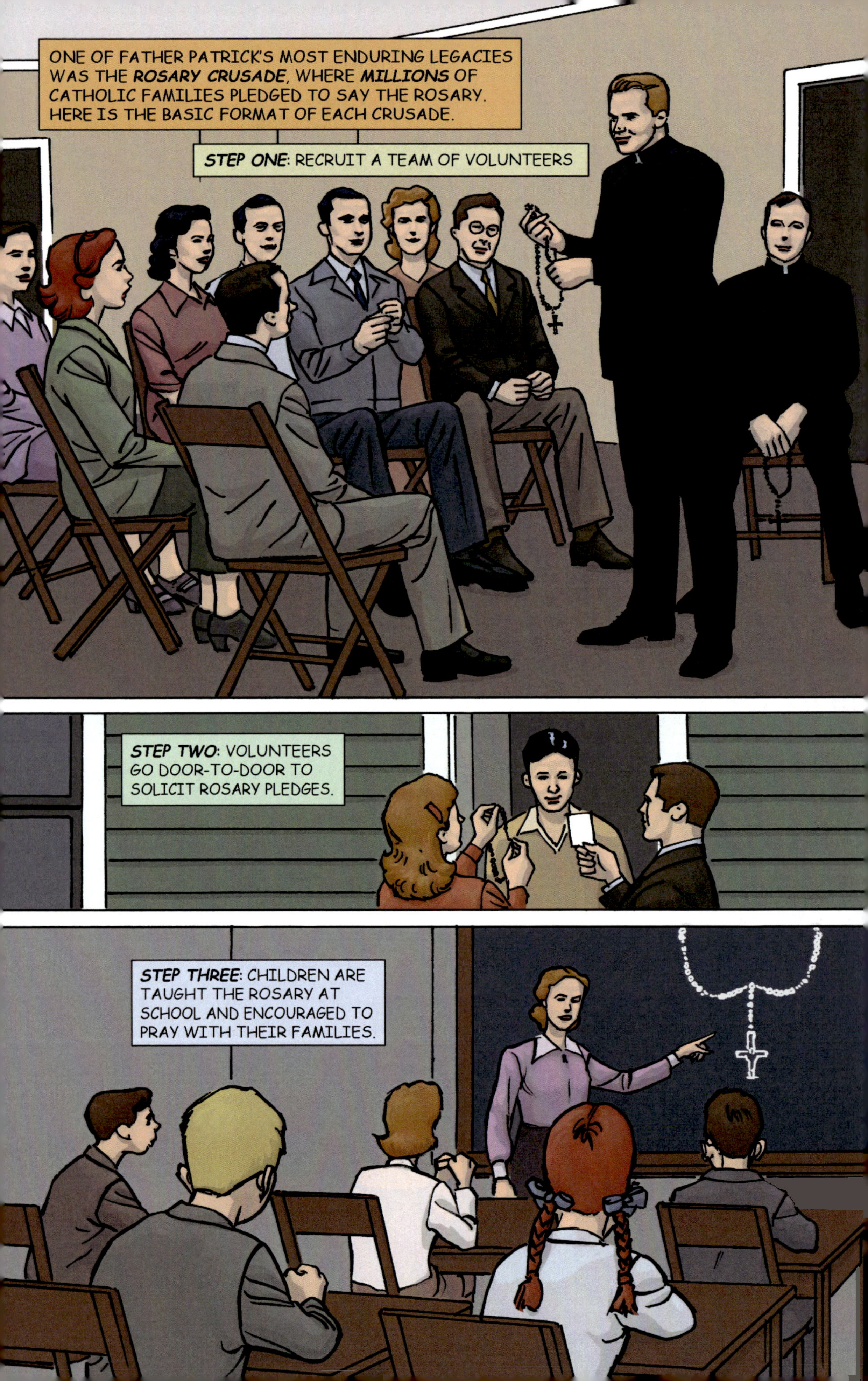

ONE OF FATHER PATRICK'S MOST ENDURING LEGACIES WAS THE ***ROSARY CRUSADE***, WHERE ***MILLIONS*** OF CATHOLIC FAMILIES PLEDGED TO SAY THE ROSARY. HERE IS THE BASIC FORMAT OF EACH CRUSADE.

STEP ONE: RECRUIT A TEAM OF VOLUNTEERS

STEP TWO: VOLUNTEERS GO DOOR-TO-DOOR TO SOLICIT ROSARY PLEDGES.

STEP FOUR: PRISONERS ARE ALSO TAUGHT THE ROSARY AND ENCOURAGED TO PLEDGE THEIR PRAYERS.

STEP FIVE: VOLUNTEERS VISIT HOSPITALS AND ASK FOR THE PRAYERS OF THE SICK AND DYING.

STEP SIX: 40 HOLY HOURS ARE PLANNED FOR THE SUCCESS OF THE ROSARY RALLY...

...AND 40 MASSES ARE OFFERED FOR THE SAME INTENTION.

THE ROSARY CRUSADE ENDS WITH A LARGE **ROSARY RALLY**.
IN RIO DE JANIERO, OVER **1.5 MILLION PEOPLE** ATTENDED THE RALLY. ONE MILLION PEOPLE ALSO PLEDGED TO PRAY THE **ROSARY** AS A FAMILY.

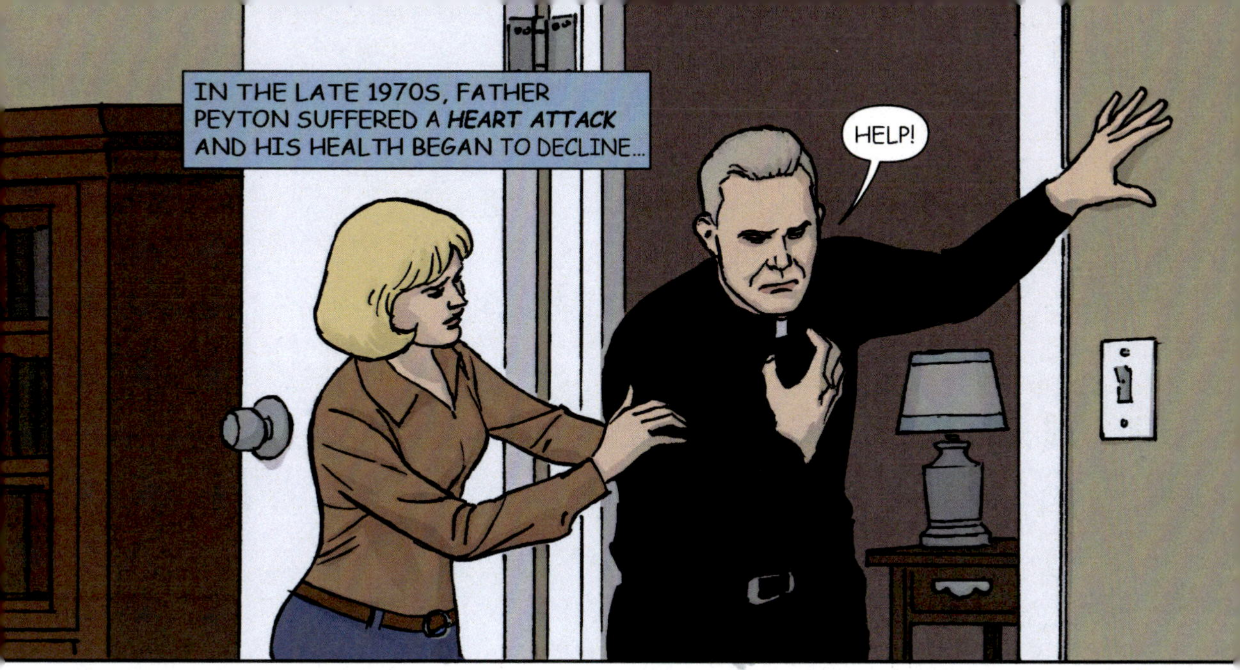

IN THE LATE 1970S, FATHER PEYTON SUFFERED A ***HEART ATTACK*** AND HIS HEALTH BEGAN TO DECLINE...

HELP!

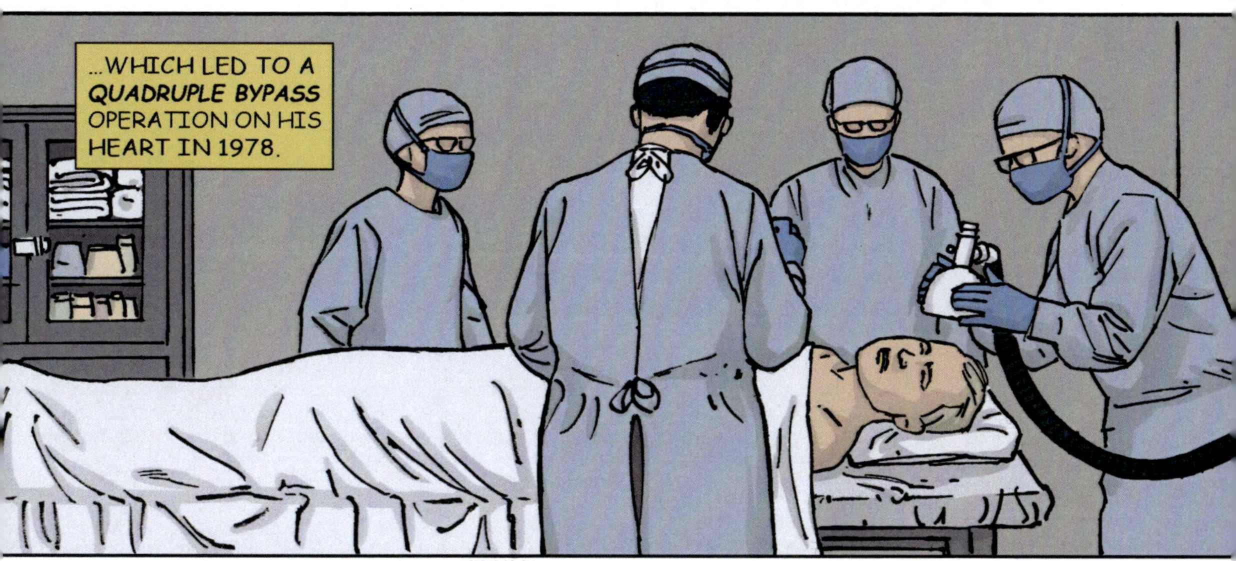

FATHER PATRICK CONTINUED TO RELY ON THE SUPPORT OF OTHER INFLUENTIAL CATHOLICS TO PROMOTE THE ROSARY.

MISSIONARIES OF CHAR

EXCUSE ME, CAN I COME IN?

COULD SOMEONE SHOW ME WHERE *MOTHER*—

WHAT IS IT, MY DEAR **FATHER PATRICK?**
COULD YOU HELP ME PROMOTE THE **ROSARY** WITH A MOVIE ABOUT THE **VISITATION?**
ANYTHING FOR **OUR LADY!**

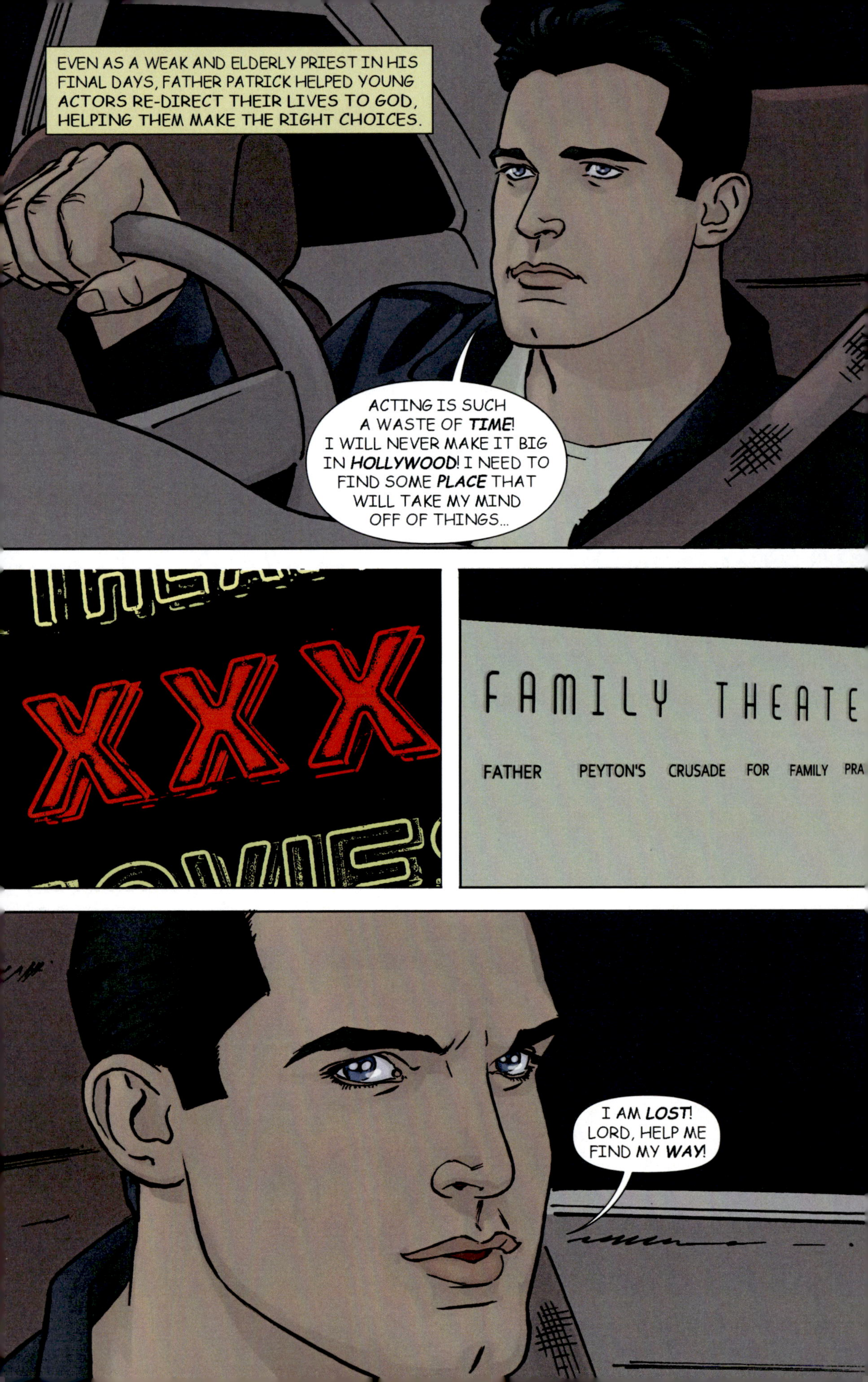

EVEN AS A WEAK AND ELDERLY PRIEST IN HIS FINAL DAYS, FATHER PATRICK HELPED YOUNG ACTORS RE-DIRECT THEIR LIVES TO GOD, HELPING THEM MAKE THE RIGHT CHOICES.

ACTING IS SUCH A WASTE OF ***TIME***! I WILL NEVER MAKE IT BIG IN ***HOLLYWOOD***! I NEED TO FIND SOME ***PLACE*** THAT WILL TAKE MY MIND OFF OF THINGS...

FAMILY THEATE

FATHER PEYTON'S CRUSADE FOR FAMILY PRA

BUZZ

FATHER, I DON'T KNOW WHO YOU ARE, BUT I AM **LOST**! WILL YOU HEAR MY **CONFESSION**?
COME IN, MY SON, LET ME HELP YOU FIND YOUR **WAY**.

YOUNG MAN, THERE ARE **BIG THINGS** IN STORE FOR YOU!
PRAY THE **ROSARY**, ATTEND **MASS** FREQUENTLY AND YOU WILL DO **GREAT THINGS**!
I **PROMISE** YOU THAT!

THANK YOU, **FATHER**, I WILL ALWAYS REMEMBER THIS **MOMENT** AND WILL TRY **NOT** TO LET YOU DOWN!
THE YOUNG MAN KEPT HIS WORD AND EVENTUALLY STARRED IN ONE OF THE MOST **ICONIC ROLES** OF THE 21ST CENTURY.

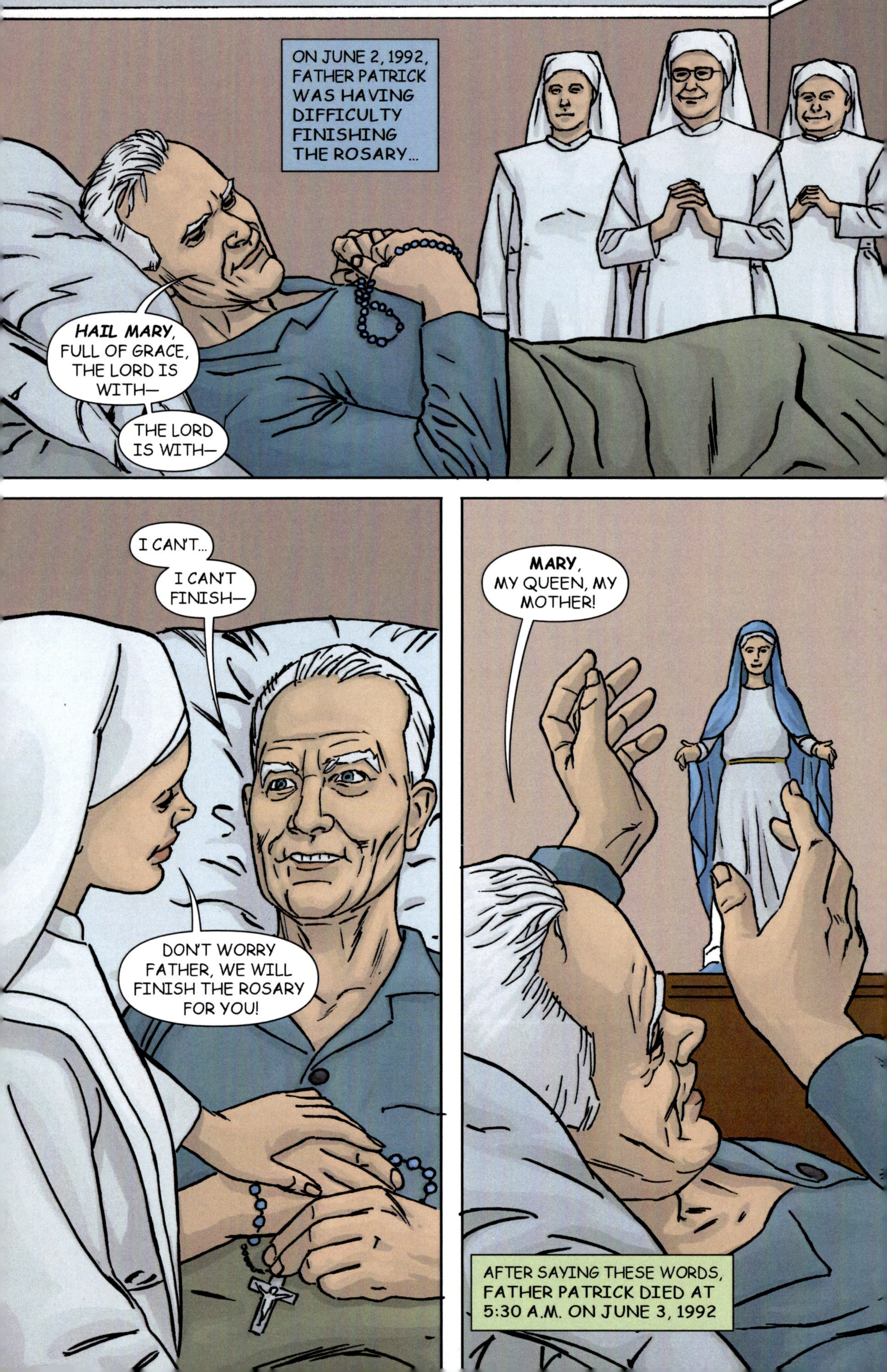

ON JUNE 2, 1992, FATHER PATRICK WAS HAVING DIFFICULTY FINISHING THE ROSARY...

HAIL MARY, FULL OF GRACE, THE LORD IS WITH—

THE LORD IS WITH—

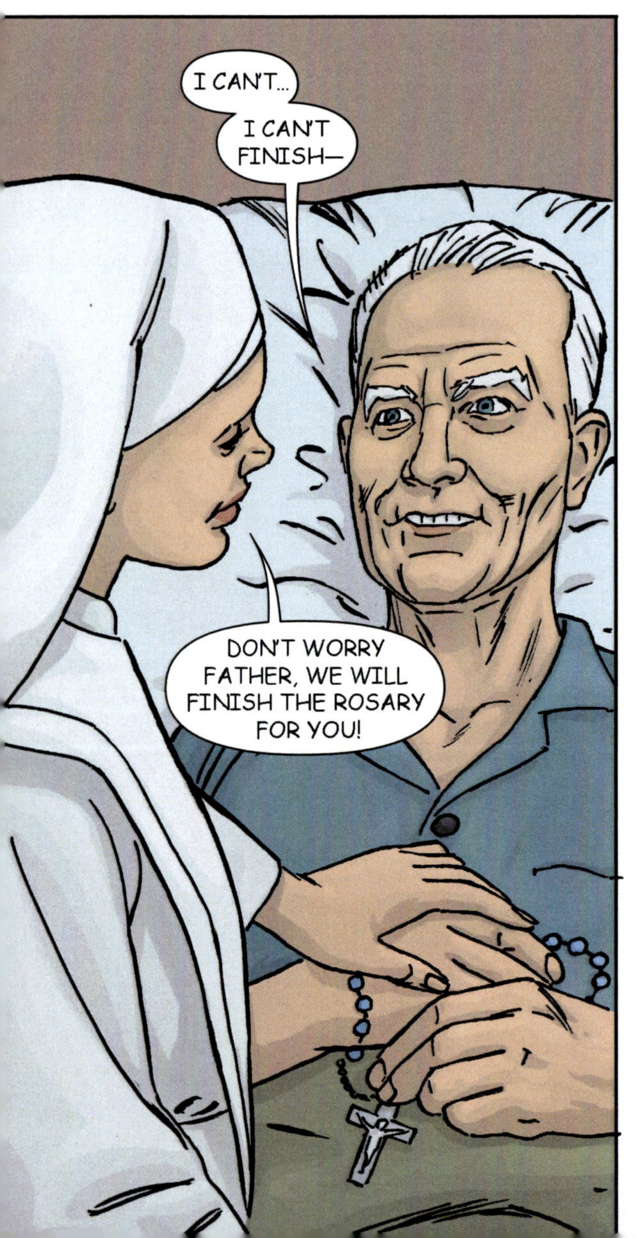

FATHER PATRICK'S LIFE HAS BEEN AN INSPIRATION TO A COUNTLESS NUMBER OF SOULS SINCE HIS DEATH. HIS LOVE FOR THE ***ROSARY*** AND ***FAMILY PRAYER*** HAS CHANGED MANY LIVES OVER THE YEARS.
IT IS HOPED THAT ONE DAY HE WILL BE RECOGNIZED AS ONE OF THE MANY SAINTS IN HEAVEN.

FATHER PATRICK PEYTON, C.S.C.
THE "ROSARY PRIEST" (1909-1992)

Strengthened by prayer and his total commitment to Our Lady, Father Peyton was able to overcome his natural shyness and in the most simple, artless, unaffected way, he convinced millions of people all over the world to commit themselves to pray the Rosary every day with their families. No one ever said that he was a great orator, but all who heard him preach could sense that he was a holy man. He radiated the love of God and inspired everyone with his simple, tender, single-minded devotion to Our Lady.

His efforts through radio, television, and film – as well as a billboard campaign that stretched across America – reached countless people with many inspirational messages, including "**The family that prays together stays together**" and "**A world at prayer is a world at peace.**"

Father Peyton never forgot his one true calling: priest in the Congregation of Holy Cross, devoted to Mary, Mother of Christ. Father Peyton offered Mass and prayed his breviary daily with great devotion. He spent long hours in prayer before the Blessed Sacrament and prayed the Rosary whenever he could free his mind from the burdens of his work. In fact, the more troublesome his problems, the more earnestly he prayed. He had committed himself to work wholeheartedly for Our Lady, not for himself, and he knew she would come to his aid. His confidence in her was unbounded and she did not disappoint him.

No matter how complex the problems of organizing huge Rosary Rallies, financing the production of movies and radio shows, traveling to distant cities and countries, or corresponding with the hundreds of people who wrote to ask for his prayers, he never lost his peace of mind or gentle manner. He never let the burdens he had to carry extinguish the love in his heart for the people he was trying to help. One lady expressed so well the experience of so many who knew him: "When he spoke to you, you felt to be embraced by his love." In fact, he manifested not only love, but also joy, peace, patience, and all the other fruits of the Spirit. He was truly a man of God. He spoke of himself as "Our Lady's donkey."

His health had never been strong and the strains of his ceaseless labors took a heavy toll on his heart. Yet even after undergoing heart surgery, he continued his labors until he was too ill to leave his room and he died under the loving care of the Little Sisters of the Poor in San Pedro, California, on June 3, 1992. His final words were, "Mary, my Queen, my Mother."

"The family is the greatest treasure the earth possesses. God is the greatest treasure of Heaven. The Rosary is the link of steel that has the power to unite them both together for time and eternity."

- Father Patrick Peyton, C.S.C.

ON THE ROAD TO BECOMING A SAINT!

THE STAGES OF CANONIZATION

- **Servant of God:** Promoter group (diocese, parish, religious congregation, etc.) requests an investigation by the Holy See; if granted, the candidate receives the title: Servant of God.
- **Venerable:** The declaration of a person's heroic virtues and sanctity of life, after which his/her title is: Venerable.
- **Blessed:** Once a miracle is attributed to the intercession of the candidate, the candidate is declared: Blessed.
- **Saint:** After a second miracle is attributed to the candidate's intercession, the Holy Father declares the candidate to be a Saint.

In **July 1997**, the first step in the Cause began. The Promoter group – the Congregation of Holy Cross – through the Postulator asked the bishop for the opening of an investigation.

In **June 2001**, A "nihil obstat" was granted from Rome and Father Peyton was given the title, **SERVANT OF GOD.**

In **November 2005**, the review of a possible medical miracle in Africa was closed and the documentation was sent to the Congregation for the Causes of Saints in Rome.

On **December 18, 2017**, Pope Francis promulgated the decree recognizing the heroic virtues of Father Patrick Peyton, a priest of the Congregation of Holy Cross, thus recognizing him as **VENERABLE** by the Roman Catholic Church.

PRAYER FOR THE BEATIFICATION OF FATHER PATRICK PEYTON, C.S.C.

Dear Jesus, Father Peyton devoted his priestly life to strengthening the families of the world by calling them to pray together every day, especially the Rosary. His message is as important for us now as it was during his life on earth. We beg You, therefore, to hasten the day of his beatification so that Your faithful people everywhere will remember his message that The Family That Prays Together Stays Together, will imitate him in his devotion to Your Mother and ours, and will be inspired by his holy life to draw ever closer to You with childlike confidence and love.

Amen.

"The family that prays together stays together."
- Father Patrick Peyton

Holy Cross Family Ministries is a family of Catholic ministries that inspires, promotes and fosters the prayer life and spiritual well-being of families throughout the world. "We help families pray!" They continue the mission of Father Patrick Peyton, C.S.C. Father Peyton believed one of God's greatest blessings is the family and he believed the best way to support the family is through prayer – particularly daily Rosary prayer. He knew that the family is the foundation of society and when the family maintains a deep and healthy mutual love, this in turn strengthens the family of the church and the entire family of humanity. Father Peyton's messages,

"The family that prays together stays together"
and
"A world at prayer is a world at peace"

continue to be the focus of all the efforts of his continuing ministry. Families are served today through Family Rosary, Family Theater Productions, Catholic Mom, the Museum of Family Prayer and the Father Peyton Family Institutes. Each ministry's unique charism provides impactful resources that strengthen families.

"We help families pray!"

Learn more at FamilyRosary.org